Lemony
CHILDREN'S STORYTELLERS
Snicket

by Chris Bowman

BLASTOFF! READERS

GRAND ISLAND PUBLIC LIBRARY

BELLWETHER MEDIA • MINNEAPOLIS, MN

Note to Librarians, Teachers, and Parents:

Blastoff! Readers are carefully developed by literacy experts and combine standards-based content with developmentally appropriate text.

Level 1 provides the most support through repetition of high-frequency words, light text, predictable sentence patterns, and strong visual support.

Level 2 offers early readers a bit more challenge through varied simple sentences, increased text load, and less repetition of high-frequency words.

Level 3 advances early-fluent readers toward fluency through increased text and concept load, less reliance on visuals, longer sentences, and more literary language.

Level 4 builds reading stamina by providing more text per page, increased use of punctuation, greater variation in sentence patterns, and increasingly challenging vocabulary.

Level 5 encourages children to move from "learning to read" to "reading to learn" by providing even more text, varied writing styles, and less familiar topics.

Whichever book is right for your reader, Blastoff! Readers are the perfect books to build confidence and encourage a love of reading that will last a lifetime!

This edition first published in 2017 by Bellwether Media, Inc.

No part of this publication may be reproduced in whole or in part without written permission of the publisher. For information regarding permission, write to Bellwether Media, Inc., Attention: Permissions Department, 5357 Penn Avenue South, Minneapolis, MN 55419.

Library of Congress Cataloging-in-Publication Data

Names: Bowman, Chris, 1990- author.
Title: Lemony Snicket / by Chris Bowman.
Description: Minneapolis, MN : Bellwether Media, Inc., 2017. | Series: Blastoff! Readers: Children's Storytellers | Includes bibliographical references and index.
Identifiers: LCCN 2016042339 (print) | LCCN 2016032039 (ebook) | ISBN 9781626175518 (hardcover : alk. paper) | ISBN 9781681032986 (ebook)
Subjects: LCSH: Snicket, Lemony–Juvenile literature. | Authors, American–21st century–Biography–Juvenile literature. | Children's stories–Authorship–Juvenile literature.
Classification: LCC PS3558.A4636 (print) | LCC PS3558.A4636 Z55 2017 (ebook) | DDC 813/.54 [B] –dc23
LC record available at https://lccn.loc.gov/2016042339

Editor: Christina Leaf   Designer: Steve Porter

Printed in the United States of America, North Mankato, MN.

Table of Contents

Lemony Snicket is the **pen name** of author Daniel Handler. He is best known as the creator of A **Series** of Unfortunate Events.

Daniel's books are wildly popular. They have been printed in more than 40 languages. More than 60 million copies have been sold worldwide!

The Young Years

Daniel Handler was born on February 28, 1970. He grew up in San Francisco, California, with his parents and younger sister, Rebecca.

San Francisco, California

N

W ✦ E

S

"I am the author of a great number of books, and I recommend none of them."
Lemony Snicket

fun fact

Daniel wrote the words for a classical music piece called *The Composer Is Dead.* It has introduced many young people to musical instruments.

Daniel had a musical childhood. He sang in an opera choir. He also learned to play the piano, accordion, and tuba.

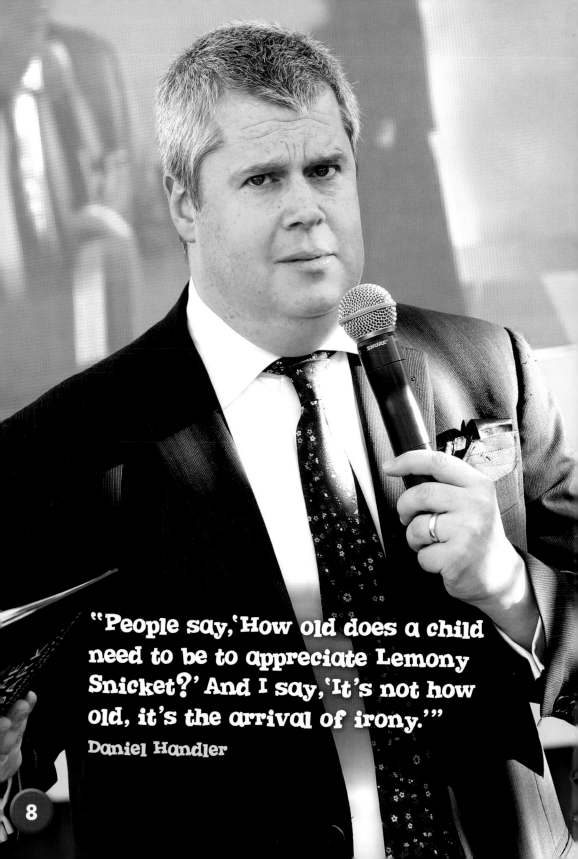

"People say,'How old does a child need to be to appreciate Lemony Snicket?' And I say,'It's not how old, it's the arrival of irony.'"

Daniel Handler

Daniel also enjoyed reading. But he was bored by the usual, happy children's books. Two of his favorite authors were Roald Dahl and Edward Gorey. Their books were dark and creepy.

Daniel's parents often read to him before bed. They would stop at an exciting moment in the story. Then they challenged him not to read any further. He usually did.

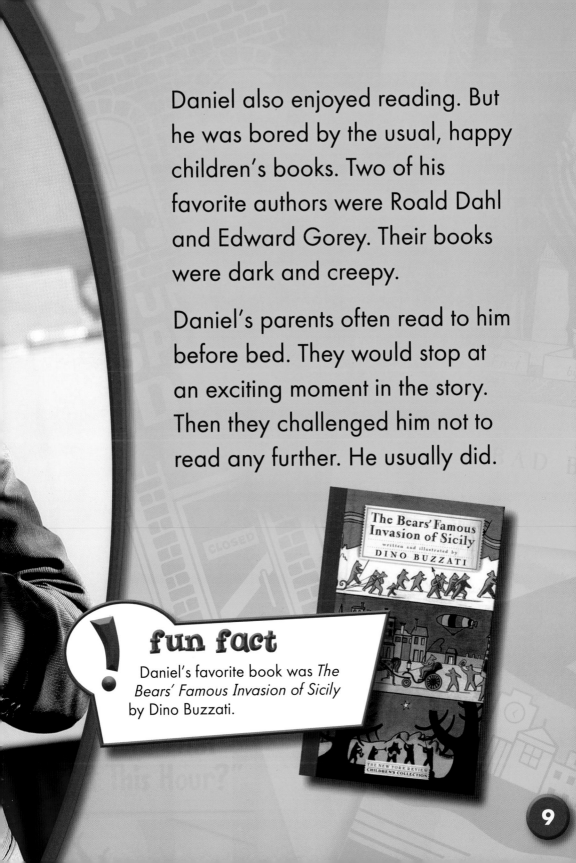

fun fact

Daniel's favorite book was *The Bears' Famous Invasion of Sicily* by Dino Buzzati.

The Productive Poet

Daniel was a bright student. After high school, he went to Connecticut for college. He focused on American Studies.

"I have always preferred stories in which mysterious and creepy things happen."
Daniel Handler

! **fun fact**

Daniel likes to keep the Lemony Snicket character mysterious. In author photos, his face is often hidden or turned away.

He also spent a lot of time writing. At first, Daniel focused on poetry. He won awards and was **encouraged** to keep writing. Soon, he started working on longer stories.

Daniel graduated from college in 1992. He worked many different jobs and wrote a **novel** in his free time. In 1998, he moved to New York. There, he tried to get his book **published**. It was **rejected** 37 times.

Finally, a publisher agreed to print Daniel's first book. *The Basic Eight* came out in 1999.

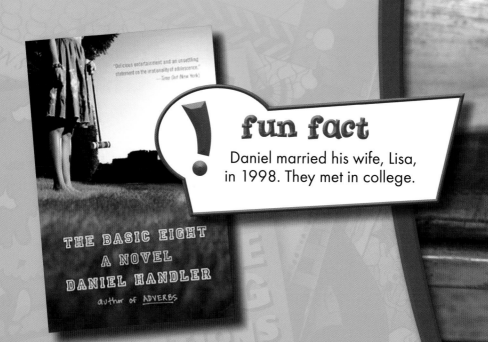

! fun fact

Daniel married his wife, Lisa, in 1998. They met in college.

Daniel was soon asked to write for young readers. He came up with a **gothic novel**. It followed a family of **orphans** whose cousin is after their money. Like the books young Daniel enjoyed, it was mysterious and often unhappy.

fun fact

Daniel usually writes books for adults using his real name. He uses the name Lemony Snicket for his books for young readers.

The Bad Beginning came out in late 1999. It was a success! Readers loved A Series of Unfortunate Events.

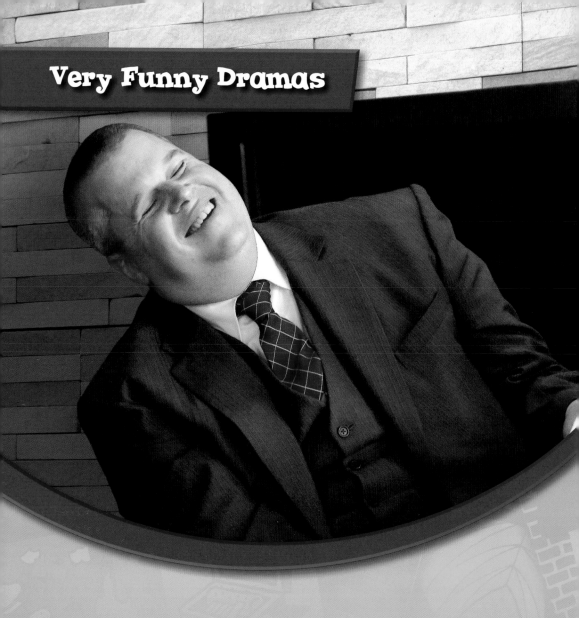

Daniel's **melodramatic** books challenge typical expectations of children's books. His stories use humor to tell sad tales. They show how bad things can happen to good people.

They also show that adults are not always good. Some, like Count Olaf, are **cruel** to the Baudelaire children. Others accidentally make bad situations worse.

SELECTED WORKS

A Series of Unfortunate Events (1999 – 2006)

The Unauthorized Autobiography (2002)

The Latke Who Wouldn't Stop Screaming (2007)

The Lump of Coal (2008)

The Composer Is Dead (2009)

13 Words (2010)

All the Wrong Questions (2012 – 2015)

The Dark (2013)

29 Myths on the Swinster Pharmacy (2014)

Daniel's books also help kids learn. They make **allusions** to famous people. Daniel also uses big words in the stories. Then he defines them in funny ways. He often does this at exciting moments in the books.

fun fact

In A Series of Unfortunate Events, the orphans are named for the famous poet Charles Baudelaire. Similarly, Mr. Poe gets his name from the poet Edgar Allan Poe.

"There is a line between people who don't know [the allusions] and people who do know them, and it's not necessarily governed by age."

Daniel Handler

POP CULTURE CONNECTION

In 2017, A Series of Unfortunate Events became a Netflix Original TV series. It features stars such as Neil Patrick Harris and Malina Weissman. They bring Count Olaf and the Baudelaire orphans to life.

However, not everyone loves Daniel's books. They have been **censored** for language and Olaf's evil plots.

The Next Novels

It has been more than ten years since Daniel wrapped up A Series of Unfortunate Events. Since then, he has written many more books for both adults and children.

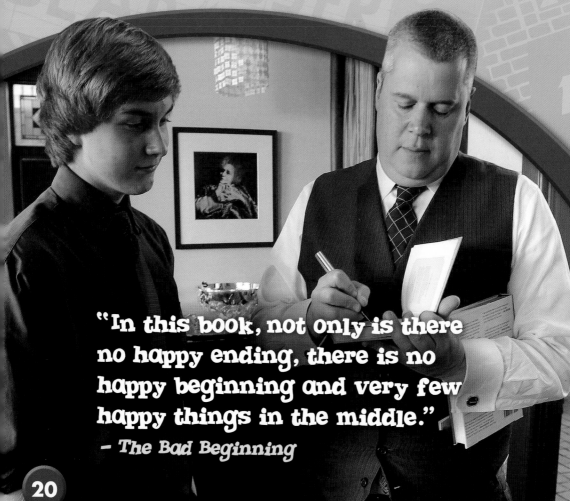

"In this book, not only is there no happy ending, there is no happy beginning and very few happy things in the middle."
– The Bad Beginning

IMPORTANT DATES

1970: Daniel Handler is born on February 28.

1990: The Academy of American Poets honors Daniel with a Poets Prize.

1992: Daniel receives the Olin Fellowship to work on his first novel.

1999: Daniel's first book, *The Basic Eight*, is published.

1999: *The Bad Beginning* becomes Daniel's first book for young readers.

2003: A Series of Unfortunate Events wins the Nickelodeon Kids' Choice Award for Favorite Book.

2004: A Series of Unfortunate Events becomes a film starring Jim Carrey.

2012: Daniel wins the Michael L. Printz Honor Book award for *Why We Broke Up*.

2014: Daniel creates the Lemony Snicket Prize for librarians.

Some of these books, the All the Wrong Questions series, are **prequels** to the first series. No matter what his name, Daniel always gives fans something new to look forward to!

Glossary

allusions—references to another person or thing

censored—removed or changed because something is considered dangerous or upsetting

cruel—ready to hurt others without feeling bad

encouraged—made more hopeful or confident

gothic novel—a type of story that is characterized by mystery, horror, and a dark setting

melodramatic—something that is so sad that it becomes funny

novel—a longer written story, usually about made-up characters and events

orphans—children whose parents have died

pen name—a name used by a writer instead of the writer's real name

prequels—stories that are set before existing works

published—printed someone's work for a public audience

rejected—turned down

series—a number of things that are connected in a certain order

To Learn More

AT THE LIBRARY

Haugen, Hayley Mitchell. *Daniel Handler: The Real Lemony Snicket*. San Diego, Calif.: KidHaven Press, 2005.

Snicket, Lemony. *The Bad Beginning*. New York, N.Y.: HarperTrophy, 2007.

Snicket, Lemony. *The Unauthorized Autobiography*. New York, N.Y.: HarperCollins, 2002.

ON THE WEB

Learning more about Lemony Snicket is as easy as 1, 2, 3.

1. Go to www.factsurfer.com.

2. Enter "Lemony Snicket" into the search box.

3. Click the "Surf" button and you will see a list of related web sites.

With factsurfer.com, finding more information is just a click away.

Index